MW00427128

IF FOUND,
PLEASE RETURN TO:

_____

_____

_____

_____

ONE LINE A DAY

A FIVE-YEAR MEMORY BOOK

CHRONICLE BOOKS
SAN FRANCISCO

ISBN 978-1-7972-1300-2

Manufactured in China.

MIX
Paper from
responsible sources
FSC™ C136333
FSC
www.fsc.org

Design by Kristen Hewitt.

10 9 8 7 6 5 4 3 2

Chronicle Books LLC
680 Second Street
San Francisco, California 94107
www.chroniclebooks.com

A CONDENSED,
COMPARATIVE
RECORD FOR
FIVE YEARS, FOR
RECORDING EVENTS
MOST WORTHY OF
REMEMBRANCE.

HOW TO USE THIS BOOK

To begin, turn to today's calendar date and fill
in the year at the top of the page's first entry.
Here, you can add your thoughts on the present
day's events. On the next day, turn the page and fill
in the year accordingly. Do likewise throughout
the year. When the year has ended, start the next
year in the second entry space on the page,
and so on through the remaining years.

JANUARY 1

20 ___ _____

_____

_____

_____

_____

20 ___ _____

_____

_____

_____

_____

20 ___ _____

_____

_____

_____

_____

20 ___ _____

_____

_____

_____

_____

20 ___ _____

_____

_____

_____

_____

JANUARY 2

20 ___ _____

_____

_____

_____

_____

20 ___ _____

_____

_____

_____

_____

20 ___ _____

_____

_____

_____

_____

20 ___ _____

_____

_____

_____

_____

20 ___ _____

_____

_____

_____

_____

JANUARY 3

20 ___ _____
_____
_____
_____
_____

20 ___ _____
_____
_____
_____
_____

20 ___ _____
_____
_____
_____
_____

20 ___ _____
_____
_____
_____
_____

20 ___ _____
_____
_____
_____
_____

JANUARY 4

20 ___ _____
_____
_____
_____
_____

20 ___ _____
_____
_____
_____
_____

20 ___ _____
_____
_____
_____
_____

20 ___ _____
_____
_____
_____
_____

20 ___ _____
_____
_____
_____
_____

JANUARY 5

20 ___ _____
_____
_____
_____
_____
_____

20 ___ _____
_____
_____
_____
_____
_____

20 ___ _____
_____
_____
_____
_____
_____

20 ___ _____
_____
_____
_____
_____
_____

20 ___ _____
_____
_____
_____
_____

JANUARY 6

20 ___ _____

20 ___ _____

20 ___ _____

20 ___ _____

20 ___ _____

JANUARY 7

20 ___ _____

_____

_____

_____

_____

20 ___ _____

_____

_____

_____

_____

20 ___ _____

_____

_____

_____

_____

20 ___ _____

_____

_____

_____

_____

20 ___ _____

_____

_____

_____

_____

JANUARY 8

20 ___ _____
_____
_____
_____
_____

20 ___ _____
_____
_____
_____
_____

20 ___ _____
_____
_____
_____
_____

20 ___ _____
_____
_____
_____
_____

20 ___ _____
_____
_____
_____
_____

JANUARY 9

20 _____ _____

_____

_____

_____

_____

_____

20 _____ _____

_____

_____

_____

_____

_____

20 _____ _____

_____

_____

_____

_____

_____

20 _____ _____

_____

_____

_____

_____

_____

20 _____ _____

_____

_____

_____

_____

_____

JANUARY 10

20 ___ _____

_____

_____

_____

_____

20 ___ _____

_____

_____

_____

_____

20 ___ _____

_____

_____

_____

_____

20 ___ _____

_____

_____

_____

_____

20 ___ _____

_____

_____

_____

_____

JANUARY 11

20 ___ _____
_____
_____
_____
_____

20 ___ _____
_____
_____
_____
_____

20 ___ _____
_____
_____
_____
_____

20 ___ _____
_____
_____
_____
_____

20 ___ _____
_____
_____
_____
_____

JANUARY 12

20 ___ _____

_____

_____

_____

_____

20 ___ _____

_____

_____

_____

_____

20 ___ _____

_____

_____

_____

_____

20 ___ _____

_____

_____

_____

_____

20 ___ _____

_____

_____

_____

_____

JANUARY 13

20 ___ _____

_____

_____

_____

_____

20 ___ _____

_____

_____

_____

_____

20 ___ _____

_____

_____

_____

_____

20 ___ _____

_____

_____

_____

_____

20 ___ _____

_____

_____

_____

_____

JANUARY 14

20 ___ _____

_____

_____

_____

_____

20 ___ _____

_____

_____

_____

_____

20 ___ _____

_____

_____

_____

_____

20 ___ _____

_____

_____

_____

_____

20 ___ _____

_____

_____

_____

_____

JANUARY 15

20 _____ _____

_____

_____

_____

_____

20 _____ _____

_____

_____

_____

_____

20 _____ _____

_____

_____

_____

_____

20 _____ _____

_____

_____

_____

_____

20 _____ _____

_____

_____

_____

_____

JANUARY 16

20 ___ _____

_____

_____

_____

_____

20 ___ _____

_____

_____

_____

_____

20 ___ _____

_____

_____

_____

_____

20 ___ _____

_____

_____

_____

_____

20 ___ _____

_____

_____

_____

_____

JANUARY 17

20 ___ _____
_____
_____
_____
_____

20 ___ _____
_____
_____
_____
_____

20 ___ _____
_____
_____
_____
_____

20 ___ _____
_____
_____
_____
_____

20 ___ _____
_____
_____
_____
_____

JANUARY 18

20 ___ _____

_____

_____

_____

_____

20 ___ _____

_____

_____

_____

_____

20 ___ _____

_____

_____

_____

_____

20 ___ _____

_____

_____

_____

_____

20 ___ _____

_____

_____

_____

_____

JANUARY 19

20 ___ _____

_____

_____

_____

_____

_____

20 ___ _____

_____

_____

_____

_____

_____

20 ___ _____

_____

_____

_____

_____

_____

20 ___ _____

_____

_____

_____

_____

_____

20 ___ _____

_____

_____

_____

_____

_____

JANUARY 20

20 ___ _____

_____

_____

_____

_____

20 ___ _____

_____

_____

_____

_____

20 ___ _____

_____

_____

_____

_____

20 ___ _____

_____

_____

_____

_____

20 ___ _____

_____

_____

_____

_____

JANUARY 21

20 ___ _____

_____
_____
_____
_____

20 ___ _____

_____
_____
_____
_____

20 ___ _____

_____
_____
_____
_____

20 ___ _____

_____
_____
_____
_____

20 ___ _____

_____
_____
_____

JANUARY 22

20 ___ _____

_____

_____

_____

_____

20 ___ _____

_____

_____

_____

_____

20 ___ _____

_____

_____

_____

_____

20 ___ _____

_____

_____

_____

_____

20 ___ _____

_____

_____

_____

_____

JANUARY 23

20 ___ _____

_____

_____

_____

_____

20 ___ _____

_____

_____

_____

_____

20 ___ _____

_____

_____

_____

_____

20 ___ _____

_____

_____

_____

_____

20 ___ _____

_____

_____

_____

_____

JANUARY 24

20 ___ _____
_____
_____
_____
_____

20 ___ _____
_____
_____
_____
_____

20 ___ _____
_____
_____
_____
_____

20 ___ _____
_____
_____
_____
_____

20 ___ _____
_____
_____
_____
_____

JANUARY 25

20 ___ _____

_____

_____

_____

_____

20 ___ _____

_____

_____

_____

_____

20 ___ _____

_____

_____

_____

_____

20 ___ _____

_____

_____

_____

_____

20 ___ _____

_____

_____

_____

_____

JANUARY 26

20 ___ _____

_____

_____

_____

_____

20 ___ _____

_____

_____

_____

_____

20 ___ _____

_____

_____

_____

_____

20 ___ _____

_____

_____

_____

_____

20 ___ _____

_____

_____

_____

_____

JANUARY 27

20 ___ _____

_____

_____

_____

_____

20 ___ _____

_____

_____

_____

_____

20 ___ _____

_____

_____

_____

_____

20 ___ _____

_____

_____

_____

_____

20 ___ _____

_____

_____

_____

_____

JANUARY 28

20 ___ _____

20 ___ _____

20 ___ _____

20 ___ _____

20 ___ _____

JANUARY 29

20 _____ _____
_____
_____
_____
_____

20 _____ _____
_____
_____
_____
_____

20 _____ _____
_____
_____
_____
_____

20 _____ _____
_____
_____
_____
_____

20 _____ _____
_____
_____
_____
_____

JANUARY 30

20 ___ _____

_____

_____

_____

_____

20 ___ _____

_____

_____

_____

_____

20 ___ _____

_____

_____

_____

_____

20 ___ _____

_____

_____

_____

_____

20 ___ _____

_____

_____

_____

_____

JANUARY 31

20 ___ _____

_____

_____

_____

_____

20 ___ _____

_____

_____

_____

_____

20 ___ _____

_____

_____

_____

_____

20 ___ _____

_____

_____

_____

_____

20 ___ _____

_____

_____

_____

_____

FEBRUARY 1

20 ___ _____

_____

_____

_____

_____

20 ___ _____

_____

_____

_____

_____

20 ___ _____

_____

_____

_____

_____

20 ___ _____

_____

_____

_____

_____

20 ___ _____

_____

_____

_____

_____

FEBRUARY 2

20 ___ _____
_____
_____
_____
_____
_____

20 ___ _____
_____
_____
_____
_____
_____

20 ___ _____
_____
_____
_____
_____
_____

20 ___ _____
_____
_____
_____
_____
_____

20 ___ _____
_____
_____
_____
_____
_____

FEBRUARY 3

20 ___ _____

_____

_____

_____

_____

20 ___ _____

_____

_____

_____

_____

20 ___ _____

_____

_____

_____

_____

20 ___ _____

_____

_____

_____

_____

20 ___ _____

_____

_____

_____

_____

FEBRUARY 4

20 ___ _____

_____

_____

_____

_____

20 ___ _____

_____

_____

_____

_____

20 ___ _____

_____

_____

_____

_____

20 ___ _____

_____

_____

_____

_____

20 ___ _____

_____

_____

_____

_____

FEBRUARY 5

20 ___ _____

20 ___ _____

20 ___ _____

20 ___ _____

20 ___ _____

FEBRUARY 6

20 ___ _____
_____
_____
_____
_____

20 ___ _____
_____
_____
_____
_____

20 ___ _____
_____
_____
_____
_____

20 ___ _____
_____
_____
_____
_____

20 ___ _____
_____
_____
_____
_____

FEBRUARY 7

20 ___ _____

20 ___ _____

20 ___ _____

20 ___ _____

20 ___ _____

FEBRUARY 8

20 ___ _____
_____
_____
_____
_____
_____

20 ___ _____
_____
_____
_____
_____
_____

20 ___ _____
_____
_____
_____
_____
_____

20 ___ _____
_____
_____
_____
_____
_____

20 ___ _____
_____
_____
_____
_____
_____

FEBRUARY 9

20 ___ _____

_____

_____

_____

_____

20 ___ _____

_____

_____

_____

_____

20 ___ _____

_____

_____

_____

_____

20 ___ _____

_____

_____

_____

_____

20 ___ _____

_____

_____

_____

_____

FEBRUARY 10

20 ___ _____

_____

_____

_____

_____

20 ___ _____

_____

_____

_____

_____

20 ___ _____

_____

_____

_____

_____

20 ___ _____

_____

_____

_____

_____

20 ___ _____

_____

_____

_____

_____

FEBRUARY 11

20 ___ _____

_____

_____

_____

_____

20 ___ _____

_____

_____

_____

_____

20 ___ _____

_____

_____

_____

_____

20 ___ _____

_____

_____

_____

_____

20 ___ _____

_____

_____

_____

_____

FEBRUARY 12

20 ___ _____

_____
_____
_____
_____

20 ___ _____

_____
_____
_____
_____

20 ___ _____

_____
_____
_____
_____

20 ___ _____

_____
_____
_____
_____

20 ___ _____

_____
_____
_____
_____

FEBRUARY 13

20 ___ _____
_____
_____
_____
_____

20 ___ _____
_____
_____
_____
_____

20 ___ _____
_____
_____
_____
_____

20 ___ _____
_____
_____
_____
_____

20 ___ _____
_____
_____
_____
_____

FEBRUARY 14

20 ___ _____
_____
_____
_____
_____

20 ___ _____
_____
_____
_____
_____

20 ___ _____
_____
_____
_____
_____

20 ___ _____
_____
_____
_____
_____

20 ___ _____
_____
_____
_____

FEBRUARY 15

20 ___ _____
_____
_____
_____
_____
_____

20 ___ _____
_____
_____
_____
_____
_____

20 ___ _____
_____
_____
_____
_____
_____

20 ___ _____
_____
_____
_____
_____
_____

20 ___ _____
_____
_____
_____
_____
_____

FEBRUARY 16

20 ___ _____

_____

_____

_____

_____

20 ___ _____

_____

_____

_____

_____

20 ___ _____

_____

_____

_____

_____

20 ___ _____

_____

_____

_____

_____

20 ___ _____

_____

_____

_____

_____

FEBRUARY 17

20 _____ _____

_____

_____

_____

_____

20 _____ _____

_____

_____

_____

_____

20 _____ _____

_____

_____

_____

_____

20 _____ _____

_____

_____

_____

_____

20 _____ _____

_____

_____

_____

_____

FEBRUARY 18

20 ___ _____
_____
_____
_____
_____

20 ___ _____
_____
_____
_____
_____

20 ___ _____
_____
_____
_____
_____

20 ___ _____
_____
_____
_____
_____

20 ___ _____
_____
_____
_____
_____

FEBRUARY 19

20 ___ _____

_____

_____

_____

_____

20 ___ _____

_____

_____

_____

_____

20 ___ _____

_____

_____

_____

_____

20 ___ _____

_____

_____

_____

_____

20 ___ _____

_____

_____

_____

_____

FEBRUARY 20

20 ___ _____
_____
_____
_____
_____

20 ___ _____
_____
_____
_____
_____

20 ___ _____
_____
_____
_____
_____

20 ___ _____
_____
_____
_____
_____

20 ___ _____
_____
_____
_____

FEBRUARY 21

20 ___ _____
_____
_____
_____
_____

20 ___ _____
_____
_____
_____
_____

20 ___ _____
_____
_____
_____
_____

20 ___ _____
_____
_____
_____
_____

20 ___ _____
_____
_____
_____
_____

FEBRUARY 22

20 ___ _____

_____

_____

_____

_____

20 ___ _____

_____

_____

_____

_____

20 ___ _____

_____

_____

_____

_____

20 ___ _____

_____

_____

_____

_____

20 ___ _____

_____

_____

_____

_____

FEBRUARY 23

20 ___ _____

_____

_____

_____

_____

20 ___ _____

_____

_____

_____

_____

20 ___ _____

_____

_____

_____

_____

20 ___ _____

_____

_____

_____

_____

20 ___ _____

_____

_____

_____

_____

FEBRUARY 24

20 ___ _____
_____
_____
_____
_____
_____

20 ___ _____
_____
_____
_____
_____
_____

20 ___ _____
_____
_____
_____
_____
_____

20 ___ _____
_____
_____
_____
_____
_____

20 ___ _____
_____
_____
_____
_____

FEBRUARY 25

20 ___ _____

_____

_____

_____

_____

20 ___ _____

_____

_____

_____

_____

20 ___ _____

_____

_____

_____

_____

20 ___ _____

_____

_____

_____

_____

20 ___ _____

_____

_____

_____

_____

FEBRUARY 26

20 ___ _____
_____
_____
_____
_____

20 ___ _____
_____
_____
_____
_____

20 ___ _____
_____
_____
_____
_____

20 ___ _____
_____
_____
_____
_____

20 ___ _____
_____
_____
_____
_____

FEBRUARY 27

20 ___ _____

_____

_____

_____

_____

20 ___ _____

_____

_____

_____

_____

20 ___ _____

_____

_____

_____

_____

20 ___ _____

_____

_____

_____

_____

20 ___ _____

_____

_____

_____

_____

FEBRUARY 28

20 ___ _____
_____
_____
_____
_____

20 ___ _____
_____
_____
_____
_____

20 ___ _____
_____
_____
_____
_____

20 ___ _____
_____
_____
_____
_____

20 ___ _____
_____
_____
_____
_____

FEBRUARY 29

20 ___ _____
_____
_____
_____
_____

20 ___ _____
_____
_____
_____
_____

20 ___ _____
_____
_____
_____
_____

20 ___ _____
_____
_____
_____
_____

20 ___ _____
_____
_____
_____
_____

MARCH 1

20 ___ _____

_____

_____

_____

_____

20 ___ _____

_____

_____

_____

_____

20 ___ _____

_____

_____

_____

_____

20 ___ _____

_____

_____

_____

_____

20 ___ _____

_____

_____

_____

_____

MARCH 2

20 ___ _____

20 ___ _____

20 ___ _____

20 ___ _____

20 ___ _____

MARCH 3

20 ___ _____

_____

_____

_____

_____

20 ___ _____

_____

_____

_____

_____

20 ___ _____

_____

_____

_____

_____

20 ___ _____

_____

_____

_____

_____

20 ___ _____

_____

_____

_____

_____

MARCH 4

20 ___ _____

_____

_____

_____

_____

_____

20 ___ _____

_____

_____

_____

_____

20 ___ _____

_____

_____

_____

_____

20 ___ _____

_____

_____

_____

_____

20 ___ _____

_____

_____

_____

_____

MARCH 5

20 ___ _____
_____
_____
_____
_____

20 ___ _____
_____
_____
_____
_____

20 ___ _____
_____
_____
_____
_____

20 ___ _____
_____
_____
_____
_____

20 ___ _____
_____
_____
_____
_____

MARCH 6

20 ___ _____

20 ___ _____

20 ___ _____

20 ___ _____

20 ___ _____

MARCH 7

20 ___ _____

_____

_____

_____

_____

20 ___ _____

_____

_____

_____

_____

20 ___ _____

_____

_____

_____

_____

20 ___ _____

_____

_____

_____

_____

20 ___ _____

_____

_____

_____

_____

MARCH 8

20 ___ _____

_____

_____

_____

_____

20 ___ _____

_____

_____

_____

_____

20 ___ _____

_____

_____

_____

_____

20 ___ _____

_____

_____

_____

_____

20 ___ _____

_____

_____

_____

_____

MARCH 9

20 ___

20 ___

20 ___

20 ___

20 ___

MARCH 10

20 __ _____

20 __ _____

20 __ _____

20 __ _____

20 __ _____

MARCH 11

20 ___ _____

20 ___ _____

20 ___ _____

20 ___ _____

20 ___ _____

MARCH 12

20 _____ _____
_____
_____
_____
_____

20 _____ _____
_____
_____
_____
_____

20 _____ _____
_____
_____
_____
_____

20 _____ _____
_____
_____
_____
_____

20 _____ _____
_____
_____
_____
_____

MARCH 13

20 ___ _____

20 ___ _____

20 ___ _____

20 ___ _____

20 ___ _____

MARCH 14

20 ___ _____

_____

_____

_____

_____

20 ___ _____

_____

_____

_____

_____

20 ___ _____

_____

_____

_____

_____

20 ___ _____

_____

_____

_____

_____

20 ___ _____

_____

_____

_____

_____

MARCH 15

20 ___ _____
_____
_____
_____
_____

20 ___ _____
_____
_____
_____
_____

20 ___ _____
_____
_____
_____
_____

20 ___ _____
_____
_____
_____
_____

20 ___ _____
_____
_____
_____
_____

MARCH 16

20 ___ _____

_____

_____

_____

_____

20 ___ _____

_____

_____

_____

_____

20 ___ _____

_____

_____

_____

_____

20 ___ _____

_____

_____

_____

_____

20 ___ _____

_____

_____

_____

_____

MARCH 17

20 ___ _____
_____
_____
_____
_____

20 ___ _____
_____
_____
_____
_____

20 ___ _____
_____
_____
_____
_____

20 ___ _____
_____
_____
_____
_____

20 ___ _____
_____
_____
_____
_____

MARCH 18

20 ___ _____

_____

_____

_____

_____

20 ___ _____

_____

_____

_____

_____

20 ___ _____

_____

_____

_____

_____

20 ___ _____

_____

_____

_____

_____

20 ___ _____

_____

_____

_____

_____

MARCH 19

20 _____ _____

_____
_____
_____
_____

20 _____ _____

_____
_____
_____
_____

20 _____ _____

_____
_____
_____
_____

20 _____ _____

_____
_____
_____
_____

20 _____ _____

_____
_____
_____
_____

MARCH 20

20 ___ _____

20 ___ _____

20 ___ _____

20 ___ _____

20 ___ _____

MARCH 21

20 ____

_____

_____

_____

_____

_____

20 ____

_____

_____

_____

_____

_____

20 ____

_____

_____

_____

_____

_____

20 ____

_____

_____

_____

_____

_____

20 ____

_____

_____

_____

_____

_____

MARCH 22

20 ___ _____

_____

_____

_____

_____

20 ___ _____

_____

_____

_____

_____

20 ___ _____

_____

_____

_____

_____

20 ___ _____

_____

_____

_____

_____

20 ___ _____

_____

_____

_____

_____

MARCH 23

20 ___ _____
_____
_____
_____
_____

20 ___ _____
_____
_____
_____
_____

20 ___ _____
_____
_____
_____
_____

20 ___ _____
_____
_____
_____
_____

20 ___ _____
_____
_____
_____
_____

MARCH 24

20 ___ _____

_____

_____

_____

_____

20 ___ _____

_____

_____

_____

_____

20 ___ _____

_____

_____

_____

_____

20 ___ _____

_____

_____

_____

_____

20 ___ _____

_____

_____

_____

_____

MARCH 25

20 ___

20 ___

20 ___

20 ___

20 ___

MARCH 26

20 ___ _____

_____

_____

_____

_____

20 ___ _____

_____

_____

_____

_____

20 ___ _____

_____

_____

_____

_____

20 ___ _____

_____

_____

_____

_____

20 ___ _____

_____

_____

_____

_____

MARCH 27

20 ___ _____

_____

_____

_____

_____

20 ___ _____

_____

_____

_____

_____

20 ___ _____

_____

_____

_____

_____

20 ___ _____

_____

_____

_____

_____

20 ___ _____

_____

_____

_____

_____

MARCH 28

20 ___ _____
_____
_____
_____
_____

20 ___ _____
_____
_____
_____
_____

20 ___ _____
_____
_____
_____
_____

20 ___ _____
_____
_____
_____
_____

20 ___ _____
_____
_____
_____
_____

MARCH 29

20 ___

_____

_____

_____

_____

_____

20 ___

_____

_____

_____

_____

_____

20 ___

_____

_____

_____

_____

_____

20 ___

_____

_____

_____

_____

_____

20 ___

_____

_____

_____

_____

_____

MARCH 30

20 ___ _____

_____

_____

_____

_____

20 ___ _____

_____

_____

_____

_____

20 ___ _____

_____

_____

_____

_____

20 ___ _____

_____

_____

_____

_____

20 ___ _____

_____

_____

_____

_____

MARCH 31

20 ___ _____

20 ___ _____

20 ___ _____

20 ___ _____

20 ___ _____

APRIL 1

20 ___ _____
_____
_____
_____
_____

20 ___ _____
_____
_____
_____
_____

20 ___ _____
_____
_____
_____
_____

20 ___ _____
_____
_____
_____
_____

20 ___ _____
_____
_____
_____
_____

APRIL 2

20 ___ _____

_____

_____

_____

_____

20 ___ _____

_____

_____

_____

_____

20 ___ _____

_____

_____

_____

_____

20 ___ _____

_____

_____

_____

_____

20 ___ _____

_____

_____

_____

_____

APRIL 3

20 ___ _____

20 ___ _____

20 ___ _____

20 ___ _____

20 ___ _____

APRIL 4

20 ___ _____

_____

_____

_____

_____

20 ___ _____

_____

_____

_____

_____

20 ___ _____

_____

_____

_____

_____

20 ___ _____

_____

_____

_____

_____

20 ___ _____

_____

_____

_____

_____

APRIL 5

20 ___ _____

_____

_____

_____

_____

20 ___ _____

_____

_____

_____

_____

20 ___ _____

_____

_____

_____

_____

20 ___ _____

_____

_____

_____

_____

20 ___ _____

_____

_____

_____

_____

APRIL 6

20 ___ _____

_____

_____

_____

_____

20 ___ _____

_____

_____

_____

_____

20 ___ _____

_____

_____

_____

_____

20 ___ _____

_____

_____

_____

_____

20 ___ _____

_____

_____

_____

_____

APRIL 7

20 ___ _____

_____

_____

_____

_____

20 ___ _____

_____

_____

_____

_____

20 ___ _____

_____

_____

_____

_____

20 ___ _____

_____

_____

_____

_____

20 ___ _____

_____

_____

_____

_____

APRIL 8

20 ___ _____

_____

_____

_____

_____

20 ___ _____

_____

_____

_____

_____

20 ___ _____

_____

_____

_____

_____

20 ___ _____

_____

_____

_____

_____

20 ___ _____

_____

_____

_____

_____

APRIL 9

20 ___ _____
_____
_____
_____
_____

20 ___ _____
_____
_____
_____
_____

20 ___ _____
_____
_____
_____
_____

20 ___ _____
_____
_____
_____
_____

20 ___ _____
_____
_____
_____
_____

APRIL 10

20 ___ _____

_____

_____

_____

_____

20 ___ _____

_____

_____

_____

_____

20 ___ _____

_____

_____

_____

_____

20 ___ _____

_____

_____

_____

_____

20 ___ _____

_____

_____

_____

_____

APRIL 11

20 ___ _____

_____

_____

_____

_____

20 ___ _____

_____

_____

_____

_____

20 ___ _____

_____

_____

_____

_____

20 ___ _____

_____

_____

_____

_____

20 ___ _____

_____

_____

_____

_____

APRIL 12

20 ___ _____

20 ___ _____

20 ___ _____

20 ___ _____

20 ___ _____

APRIL 13

20 ___ _____
_____
_____
_____
_____

20 ___ _____
_____
_____
_____
_____

20 ___ _____
_____
_____
_____
_____

20 ___ _____
_____
_____
_____
_____

20 ___ _____
_____
_____
_____
_____

APRIL 14

20 ___ _____

_____

_____

_____

_____

20 ___ _____

_____

_____

_____

_____

20 ___ _____

_____

_____

_____

_____

20 ___ _____

_____

_____

_____

_____

20 ___ _____

_____

_____

_____

_____

APRIL 15

20 ___ _____

_____

_____

_____

_____

20 ___ _____

_____

_____

_____

_____

20 ___ _____

_____

_____

_____

_____

20 ___ _____

_____

_____

_____

_____

20 ___ _____

_____

_____

_____

_____

APRIL 16

20 ___ _____

_____

_____

_____

_____

20 ___ _____

_____

_____

_____

_____

20 ___ _____

_____

_____

_____

_____

20 ___ _____

_____

_____

_____

_____

20 ___ _____

_____

_____

_____

_____

APRIL 17

20 ___ _____

_____

_____

_____

_____

20 ___ _____

_____

_____

_____

_____

20 ___ _____

_____

_____

_____

_____

20 ___ _____

_____

_____

_____

_____

20 ___ _____

_____

_____

_____

_____

APRIL 18

20 ___ _____

_____

_____

_____

_____

20 ___ _____

_____

_____

_____

_____

20 ___ _____

_____

_____

_____

_____

20 ___ _____

_____

_____

_____

_____

20 ___ _____

_____

_____

_____

_____

APRIL 19

20 ___ _____

_____

_____

_____

_____

20 ___ _____

_____

_____

_____

_____

20 ___ _____

_____

_____

_____

_____

20 ___ _____

_____

_____

_____

_____

20 ___ _____

_____

_____

_____

_____

APRIL 20

20 ___ _____
_____
_____
_____
_____
_____

20 ___ _____
_____
_____
_____
_____
_____

20 ___ _____
_____
_____
_____
_____
_____

20 ___ _____
_____
_____
_____
_____
_____

20 ___ _____
_____
_____
_____
_____

APRIL 21

20 ___ _____

_____

_____

_____

_____

20 ___ _____

_____

_____

_____

_____

20 ___ _____

_____

_____

_____

_____

20 ___ _____

_____

_____

_____

_____

20 ___ _____

_____

_____

_____

_____

APRIL 22

20 ___ _____

_____

_____

_____

_____

20 ___ _____

_____

_____

_____

_____

20 ___ _____

_____

_____

_____

_____

20 ___ _____

_____

_____

_____

_____

20 ___ _____

_____

_____

_____

_____

APRIL 23

20 ___ _____

_____

_____

_____

_____

20 ___ _____

_____

_____

_____

_____

20 ___ _____

_____

_____

_____

_____

20 ___ _____

_____

_____

_____

_____

20 ___ _____

_____

_____

_____

_____

APRIL 24

20 ___ _____
_____
_____
_____
_____

20 ___ _____
_____
_____
_____
_____

20 ___ _____
_____
_____
_____
_____

20 ___ _____
_____
_____
_____
_____

20 ___ _____
_____
_____
_____
_____

APRIL 25

20 ___ _____

_____

_____

_____

_____

20 ___ _____

_____

_____

_____

_____

20 ___ _____

_____

_____

_____

_____

20 ___ _____

_____

_____

_____

_____

20 ___ _____

_____

_____

_____

_____

APRIL 26

20 _____ _____

_____

_____

_____

_____

20 _____ _____

_____

_____

_____

_____

20 _____ _____

_____

_____

_____

_____

20 _____ _____

_____

_____

_____

_____

20 _____ _____

_____

_____

_____

_____

APRIL 27

20 ___ _____

_____

_____

_____

_____

20 ___ _____

_____

_____

_____

_____

20 ___ _____

_____

_____

_____

_____

20 ___ _____

_____

_____

_____

_____

20 ___ _____

_____

_____

_____

_____

APRIL 28

20 ___ _____

_____

_____

_____

_____

_____

20 ___ _____

_____

_____

_____

_____

_____

20 ___ _____

_____

_____

_____

_____

_____

20 ___ _____

_____

_____

_____

_____

20 ___ _____

_____

_____

_____

_____

APRIL 29

20 ___ _____

_____

_____

_____

_____

20 ___ _____

_____

_____

_____

_____

20 ___ _____

_____

_____

_____

_____

20 ___ _____

_____

_____

_____

_____

20 ___ _____

_____

_____

_____

_____

APRIL 30

20 ___ _____

_____

_____

_____

_____

20 ___ _____

_____

_____

_____

_____

20 ___ _____

_____

_____

_____

_____

20 ___ _____

_____

_____

_____

_____

20 ___ _____

_____

_____

_____

_____

MAY 1

20 ___ _____
_____
_____
_____
_____

20 ___ _____
_____
_____
_____
_____

20 ___ _____
_____
_____
_____
_____

20 ___ _____
_____
_____
_____
_____

20 ___ _____
_____
_____
_____
_____

MAY 2

20 ___ _____

_____

_____

_____

_____

20 ___ _____

_____

_____

_____

_____

20 ___ _____

_____

_____

_____

_____

20 ___ _____

_____

_____

_____

_____

20 ___ _____

_____

_____

_____

_____

MAY 3

20 ___ _____

20 ___ _____

20 ___ _____

20 ___ _____

20 ___ _____

MAY 4

20 ___ _____

_____

_____

_____

_____

20 ___ _____

_____

_____

_____

_____

20 ___ _____

_____

_____

_____

_____

20 ___ _____

_____

_____

_____

_____

20 ___ _____

_____

_____

_____

_____

MAY 5

20 ___ _____

20 ___ _____

20 ___ _____

20 ___ _____

20 ___ _____

MAY 6

20 ___ _____

_____

_____

_____

_____

20 ___ _____

_____

_____

_____

_____

20 ___ _____

_____

_____

_____

_____

20 ___ _____

_____

_____

_____

_____

20 ___ _____

_____

_____

_____

_____

MAY 7

20 _____ _____

_____

_____

_____

_____

20 _____ _____

_____

_____

_____

_____

20 _____ _____

_____

_____

_____

_____

20 _____ _____

_____

_____

_____

_____

20 _____ _____

_____

_____

_____

_____

MAY 8

20 ___ _____

20 ___ _____

20 ___ _____

20 ___ _____

20 ___ _____

MAY 9

20 ___ _____

20 ___ _____

20 ___ _____

20 ___ _____

20 ___ _____

MAY 10

20 ___ _____

_____

_____

_____

_____

20 ___ _____

_____

_____

_____

_____

20 ___ _____

_____

_____

_____

_____

20 ___ _____

_____

_____

_____

_____

20 ___ _____

_____

_____

_____

_____

MAY 11

20 ___ _____

_____

_____

_____

_____

20 ___ _____

_____

_____

_____

_____

20 ___ _____

_____

_____

_____

_____

20 ___ _____

_____

_____

_____

_____

20 ___ _____

_____

_____

_____

_____

MAY 12

20 ___ _____

_____

_____

_____

_____

20 ___ _____

_____

_____

_____

_____

20 ___ _____

_____

_____

_____

_____

20 ___ _____

_____

_____

_____

_____

20 ___ _____

_____

_____

_____

_____

MAY 13

20 ___ _____

_____

_____

_____

_____

20 ___ _____

_____

_____

_____

_____

20 ___ _____

_____

_____

_____

_____

20 ___ _____

_____

_____

_____

_____

20 ___ _____

_____

_____

_____

_____

MAY 14

20 ___ _____

20 ___ _____

20 ___ _____

20 ___ _____

20 ___ _____

MAY 15

20 ___ _____
_____
_____
_____
_____

20 ___ _____
_____
_____
_____
_____

20 ___ _____
_____
_____
_____
_____

20 ___ _____
_____
_____
_____
_____

20 ___ _____
_____
_____
_____
_____

MAY 16

20 ___ _____

20 ___ _____

20 ___ _____

20 ___ _____

20 ___ _____

MAY 17

20 ___ _____

_____

_____

_____

_____

20 ___ _____

_____

_____

_____

_____

20 ___ _____

_____

_____

_____

_____

20 ___ _____

_____

_____

_____

_____

20 ___ _____

_____

_____

_____

_____

MAY 18

20 ___ _____

20 ___ _____

20 ___ _____

20 ___ _____

20 ___ _____

MAY 19

20 ___ _____

_____

_____

_____

_____

20 ___ _____

_____

_____

_____

_____

20 ___ _____

_____

_____

_____

_____

20 ___ _____

_____

_____

_____

_____

20 ___ _____

_____

_____

_____

_____

MAY 20

20 ___ _____

20 ___ _____

20 ___ _____

20 ___ _____

20 ___ _____

MAY 21

20 ___ _____

20 ___ _____

20 ___ _____

20 ___ _____

20 ___ _____

MAY 22

20 ___ _____
_____
_____
_____
_____

20 ___ _____
_____
_____
_____
_____

20 ___ _____
_____
_____
_____

20 ___ _____
_____
_____
_____
_____

20 ___ _____
_____
_____
_____
_____

MAY 23

20 ___ _____

_____

_____

_____

_____

20 ___ _____

_____

_____

_____

_____

20 ___ _____

_____

_____

_____

_____

20 ___ _____

_____

_____

_____

_____

20 ___ _____

_____

_____

_____

_____

MAY 24

20 ___

_____

20 ___

_____

20 ___

_____

20 ___

_____

20 ___

_____

MAY 25

20 ___ _____

_____

_____

_____

_____

20 ___ _____

_____

_____

_____

_____

20 ___ _____

_____

_____

_____

_____

20 ___ _____

_____

_____

_____

_____

20 ___ _____

_____

_____

_____

_____

MAY 26

20 ___ _____

_____

_____

_____

_____

20 ___ _____

_____

_____

_____

_____

20 ___ _____

_____

_____

_____

_____

20 ___ _____

_____

_____

_____

_____

20 ___ _____

_____

_____

_____

_____

MAY 27

20 ___ _____

_____

_____

_____

_____

20 ___ _____

_____

_____

_____

_____

20 ___ _____

_____

_____

_____

_____

20 ___ _____

_____

_____

_____

_____

20 ___ _____

_____

_____

_____

_____

MAY 28

20 ___ _____

20 ___ _____

20 ___ _____

20 ___ _____

20 ___ _____

MAY 29

20 ___ _____
_____
_____
_____
_____

20 ___ _____
_____
_____
_____
_____

20 ___ _____
_____
_____
_____
_____

20 ___ _____
_____
_____
_____
_____

20 ___ _____
_____
_____
_____
_____

MAY 30

20 _____ _____

20 _____ _____

20 _____ _____

20 _____ _____

20 _____ _____

MAY 31

20 ___ _____

20 ___ _____

20 ___ _____

20 ___ _____

20 ___ _____

JUNE 1

20 ___ _____

20 ___ _____

20 ___ _____

20 ___ _____

20 ___ _____

JUNE 2

20 ___ _____

20 ___ _____

20 ___ _____

20 ___ _____

20 ___ _____

JUNE 3

20 ___ _____

20 ___ _____

20 ___ _____

20 ___ _____

20 ___ _____

JUNE 4

20 ___

___

20 ___

___

20 ___

___

20 ___

___

20 ___

___

JUNE 5

20 ___ _____

_____

_____

_____

_____

20 ___ _____

_____

_____

_____

_____

20 ___ _____

_____

_____

_____

_____

20 ___ _____

_____

_____

_____

_____

20 ___ _____

_____

_____

_____

_____

JUNE 6

20 ___ _____

20 ___ _____

20 ___ _____

20 ___ _____

20 ___ _____

JUNE 7

20 ___ _____

_____

_____

_____

_____

20 ___ _____

_____

_____

_____

_____

20 ___ _____

_____

_____

_____

_____

20 ___ _____

_____

_____

_____

_____

20 ___ _____

_____

_____

_____

_____

JUNE 8

20 ___ _____

_____

_____

_____

_____

20 ___ _____

_____

_____

_____

_____

20 ___ _____

_____

_____

_____

_____

20 ___ _____

_____

_____

_____

_____

20 ___ _____

_____

_____

_____

_____

JUNE 9

20 ___ _____

_____

_____

_____

_____

20 ___ _____

_____

_____

_____

_____

20 ___ _____

_____

_____

_____

_____

20 ___ _____

_____

_____

_____

_____

20 ___ _____

_____

_____

_____

_____

JUNE 10

20 ___ _____

20 ___ _____

20 ___ _____

20 ___ _____

20 ___ _____

JUNE 11

20 ___ _____

20 ___ _____

20 ___ _____

20 ___ _____

20 ___ _____

JUNE 12

20 ___ _____

_____

_____

_____

_____

20 ___ _____

_____

_____

_____

_____

20 ___ _____

_____

_____

_____

_____

20 ___ _____

_____

_____

_____

_____

20 ___ _____

_____

_____

_____

_____

JUNE 13

20 ___ _____

_____

_____

_____

_____

20 ___ _____

_____

_____

_____

_____

20 ___ _____

_____

_____

_____

_____

20 ___ _____

_____

_____

_____

_____

20 ___ _____

_____

_____

_____

_____

JUNE 14

20 ___ _____

_____

_____

_____

_____

20 ___ _____

_____

_____

_____

_____

20 ___ _____

_____

_____

_____

_____

20 ___ _____

_____

_____

_____

_____

20 ___ _____

_____

_____

_____

_____

JUNE 15

20 ___ _____

_____

_____

_____

_____

20 ___ _____

_____

_____

_____

_____

20 ___ _____

_____

_____

_____

_____

20 ___ _____

_____

_____

_____

_____

20 ___ _____

_____

_____

_____

_____

JUNE 16

20 _____ _____

20 _____ _____

20 _____ _____

20 _____ _____

20 _____ _____

JUNE 17

20 ___ _____
_____
_____
_____
_____

20 ___ _____
_____
_____
_____
_____

20 ___ _____
_____
_____
_____
_____

20 ___ _____
_____
_____
_____
_____

20 ___ _____
_____
_____
_____
_____

JUNE 18

20 ___ _____

20 ___ _____

20 ___ _____

20 ___ _____

20 ___ _____

JUNE 19

20 _____ _____

_____

_____

_____

_____

20 _____ _____

_____

_____

_____

_____

20 _____ _____

_____

_____

_____

_____

20 _____ _____

_____

_____

_____

_____

20 _____ _____

_____

_____

_____

_____

JUNE 20

20 ___ _____

_____

_____

_____

_____

_____

20 ___ _____

_____

_____

_____

_____

_____

20 ___ _____

_____

_____

_____

_____

_____

20 ___ _____

_____

_____

_____

_____

_____

20 ___ _____

_____

_____

_____

_____

JUNE 21

20 ___ _____

_____

_____

_____

_____

20 ___ _____

_____

_____

_____

_____

20 ___ _____

_____

_____

_____

_____

20 ___ _____

_____

_____

_____

_____

20 ___ _____

_____

_____

_____

_____

JUNE 22

20 ___ _____

20 ___ _____

20 ___ _____

20 ___ _____

20 ___ _____

JUNE 23

20 ___ _____

_____

_____

_____

_____

20 ___ _____

_____

_____

_____

_____

20 ___ _____

_____

_____

_____

_____

20 ___ _____

_____

_____

_____

_____

20 ___ _____

_____

_____

_____

_____

JUNE 24

20 ___ _____

20 ___ _____

20 ___ _____

20 ___ _____

20 ___ _____

JUNE 25

20 ___ _____

20 ___ _____

20 ___ _____

20 ___ _____

20 ___ _____

JUNE 26

20 ___ _____

_____
_____
_____
_____

20 ___ _____

_____
_____
_____
_____

20 ___ _____

_____
_____
_____
_____

20 ___ _____

_____
_____
_____
_____

20 ___ _____

_____
_____
_____
_____

JUNE 27

20 ___ _____

_____

_____

_____

_____

20 ___ _____

_____

_____

_____

_____

20 ___ _____

_____

_____

_____

_____

20 ___ _____

_____

_____

_____

_____

20 ___ _____

_____

_____

_____

_____

JUNE 28

20 ___ _____

20 ___ _____

20 ___ _____

20 ___ _____

20 ___ _____

JUNE 29

20 ___ _____

_____

_____

_____

_____

20 ___ _____

_____

_____

_____

_____

20 ___ _____

_____

_____

_____

_____

20 ___ _____

_____

_____

_____

_____

20 ___ _____

_____

_____

_____

_____

JUNE 30

20 ___ _____

_____

_____

_____

_____

20 ___ _____

_____

_____

_____

_____

20 ___ _____

_____

_____

_____

_____

20 ___ _____

_____

_____

_____

_____

20 ___ _____

_____

_____

_____

_____

JULY 1

20 ___ _____

_____

_____

_____

_____

20 ___ _____

_____

_____

_____

_____

20 ___ _____

_____

_____

_____

20 ___ _____

_____

_____

_____

_____

20 ___ _____

_____

_____

_____

_____

JULY 2

20 ___ _____

20 ___ _____

20 ___ _____

20 ___ _____

20 ___ _____

JULY 3

20 ___ _____

_____

_____

_____

_____

20 ___ _____

_____

_____

_____

_____

20 ___ _____

_____

_____

_____

_____

20 ___ _____

_____

_____

_____

_____

20 ___ _____

_____

_____

_____

_____

JULY 4

20 ___ _____

_____

_____

_____

_____

20 ___ _____

_____

_____

_____

_____

20 ___ _____

_____

_____

_____

_____

20 ___ _____

_____

_____

_____

_____

20 ___ _____

_____

_____

_____

_____

JULY 5

20 ___ _____

20 ___ _____

20 ___ _____

20 ___ _____

20 ___ _____

JULY 6

20 ___ _____

20 ___ _____

20 ___ _____

20 ___ _____

20 ___ _____

JULY 7

20 ___ _____

_____

_____

_____

_____

20 ___ _____

_____

_____

_____

_____

20 ___ _____

_____

_____

_____

_____

20 ___ _____

_____

_____

_____

_____

20 ___ _____

_____

_____

_____

_____

JULY 8

20 ___ _____

_____

_____

_____

_____

20 ___ _____

_____

_____

_____

_____

20 ___ _____

_____

_____

_____

_____

20 ___ _____

_____

_____

_____

_____

20 ___ _____

_____

_____

_____

_____

JULY 9

20 ___ _____

_____

_____

_____

_____

20 ___ _____

_____

_____

_____

_____

20 ___ _____

_____

_____

_____

_____

20 ___ _____

_____

_____

_____

_____

20 ___ _____

_____

_____

_____

_____

JULY 10

20 ___ _____

20 ___ _____

20 ___ _____

20 ___ _____

20 ___ _____

JULY 11

20 ___ _____
_____
_____
_____
_____

20 ___ _____
_____
_____
_____
_____

20 ___ _____
_____
_____
_____
_____

20 ___ _____
_____
_____
_____
_____

20 ___ _____
_____
_____
_____
_____

JULY 12

20 ___ _____

20 ___ _____

20 ___ _____

20 ___ _____

20 ___ _____

JULY 13

20 ___

20 ___

20 ___

20 ___

20 ___

JULY 14

20 ___ _____

_____

_____

_____

_____

20 ___ _____

_____

_____

_____

_____

20 ___ _____

_____

_____

_____

_____

20 ___ _____

_____

_____

_____

_____

20 ___ _____

_____

_____

_____

_____

JULY 15

20 ___ _____

20 ___ _____

20 ___ _____

20 ___ _____

20 ___ _____

JULY 16

20 ___ _____

_____

_____

_____

_____

_____

20 ___ _____

_____

_____

_____

_____

_____

20 ___ _____

_____

_____

_____

_____

_____

20 ___ _____

_____

_____

_____

_____

_____

20 ___ _____

_____

_____

_____

_____

_____

JULY 17

20 ___ _____

_____

_____

_____

_____

20 ___ _____

_____

_____

_____

_____

20 ___ _____

_____

_____

_____

_____

20 ___ _____

_____

_____

_____

_____

20 ___ _____

_____

_____

_____

_____

JULY 18

20 ___ _____

_____

_____

_____

_____

20 ___ _____

_____

_____

_____

_____

20 ___ _____

_____

_____

_____

_____

20 ___ _____

_____

_____

_____

_____

20 ___ _____

_____

_____

_____

_____

JULY 19

20 ___ _____

_____

_____

_____

_____

20 ___ _____

_____

_____

_____

_____

20 ___ _____

_____

_____

_____

_____

20 ___ _____

_____

_____

_____

_____

20 ___ _____

_____

_____

_____

_____

JULY 20

20 ___ _____

_____

_____

_____

_____

20 ___ _____

_____

_____

_____

_____

20 ___ _____

_____

_____

_____

_____

20 ___ _____

_____

_____

_____

_____

20 ___ _____

_____

_____

_____

_____

JULY 21

20 ___ _____

_____

_____

_____

_____

_____

20 ___ _____

_____

_____

_____

_____

_____

20 ___ _____

_____

_____

_____

_____

_____

20 ___ _____

_____

_____

_____

_____

_____

20 ___ _____

_____

_____

_____

_____

_____

JULY 22

20 ___ _____

_____

_____

_____

_____

20 ___ _____

_____

_____

_____

_____

20 ___ _____

_____

_____

_____

_____

20 ___ _____

_____

_____

_____

_____

20 ___ _____

_____

_____

_____

_____

JULY 23

20 ___ _____

_____

_____

_____

_____

20 ___ _____

_____

_____

_____

_____

20 ___ _____

_____

_____

_____

_____

20 ___ _____

_____

_____

_____

_____

20 ___ _____

_____

_____

_____

_____

JULY 24

20 ___ _____

_____

_____

_____

_____

20 ___ _____

_____

_____

_____

_____

20 ___ _____

_____

_____

_____

_____

20 ___ _____

_____

_____

_____

_____

20 ___ _____

_____

_____

_____

_____

JULY 25

20 ___ _____

_____

_____

_____

_____

20 ___ _____

_____

_____

_____

_____

20 ___ _____

_____

_____

_____

_____

20 ___ _____

_____

_____

_____

_____

20 ___ _____

_____

_____

_____

_____

JULY 26

20 ___ _____

_____

_____

_____

_____

20 ___ _____

_____

_____

_____

_____

20 ___ _____

_____

_____

_____

_____

20 ___ _____

_____

_____

_____

_____

20 ___ _____

_____

_____

_____

_____

JULY 27

20 ___ _____

_____

_____

_____

_____

20 ___ _____

_____

_____

_____

_____

20 ___ _____

_____

_____

_____

_____

20 ___ _____

_____

_____

_____

_____

20 ___ _____

_____

_____

_____

_____

JULY 28

20 ___ _____

20 ___ _____

20 ___ _____

20 ___ _____

20 ___ _____

JULY 29

20 ___ _____

_____

_____

_____

_____

20 ___ _____

_____

_____

_____

_____

20 ___ _____

_____

_____

_____

_____

20 ___ _____

_____

_____

_____

_____

20 ___ _____

_____

_____

_____

_____

JULY 30

20 ___ _____

20 ___ _____

20 ___ _____

20 ___ _____

20 ___ _____

JULY 31

20 ___ _____

_____

_____

_____

_____

20 ___ _____

_____

_____

_____

_____

20 ___ _____

_____

_____

_____

_____

20 ___ _____

_____

_____

_____

_____

20 ___ _____

_____

_____

_____

_____

AUGUST 1

20 ___ _____

_____

_____

_____

_____

20 ___ _____

_____

_____

_____

_____

20 ___ _____

_____

_____

_____

_____

20 ___ _____

_____

_____

_____

_____

20 ___ _____

_____

_____

_____

_____

AUGUST 2

20 ___ _____
_____
_____
_____
_____

20 ___ _____
_____
_____
_____
_____

20 ___ _____
_____
_____
_____
_____

20 ___ _____
_____
_____
_____
_____

20 ___ _____
_____
_____
_____
_____

AUGUST 3

20 ___ _____

_____

_____

_____

_____

20 ___ _____

_____

_____

_____

_____

20 ___ _____

_____

_____

_____

_____

20 ___ _____

_____

_____

_____

_____

20 ___ _____

_____

_____

_____

_____

AUGUST 4

20 ___ _____

_____

_____

_____

_____

20 ___ _____

_____

_____

_____

_____

20 ___ _____

_____

_____

_____

_____

20 ___ _____

_____

_____

_____

_____

20 ___ _____

_____

_____

_____

_____

AUGUST 5

20 ___ _____

_____

_____

_____

_____

20 ___ _____

_____

_____

_____

_____

20 ___ _____

_____

_____

_____

_____

20 ___ _____

_____

_____

_____

_____

20 ___ _____

_____

_____

_____

_____

AUGUST 6

20 ___ _____

_____

_____

_____

_____

20 ___ _____

_____

_____

_____

_____

20 ___ _____

_____

_____

_____

_____

20 ___ _____

_____

_____

_____

_____

20 ___ _____

_____

_____

_____

_____

AUGUST 7

20 ___ _____

20 ___ _____

20 ___ _____

20 ___ _____

20 ___ _____

AUGUST 8

20 ___ _____

_____

_____

_____

_____

20 ___ _____

_____

_____

_____

_____

20 ___ _____

_____

_____

_____

_____

20 ___ _____

_____

_____

_____

_____

20 ___ _____

_____

_____

_____

_____

AUGUST 9

20 ___ _____

_____

_____

_____

_____

20 ___ _____

_____

_____

_____

_____

20 ___ _____

_____

_____

_____

_____

20 ___ _____

_____

_____

_____

_____

20 ___ _____

_____

_____

_____

_____

AUGUST 10

20 ___ _____

_____

_____

_____

_____

20 ___ _____

_____

_____

_____

_____

20 ___ _____

_____

_____

_____

_____

20 ___ _____

_____

_____

_____

_____

20 ___ _____

_____

_____

_____

_____

AUGUST 11

20 ___ _____

_____

_____

_____

_____

20 ___ _____

_____

_____

_____

_____

20 ___ _____

_____

_____

_____

_____

20 ___ _____

_____

_____

_____

_____

20 ___ _____

_____

_____

_____

_____

AUGUST 12

20 ___ _____

20 ___ _____

20 ___ _____

20 ___ _____

20 ___ _____

AUGUST 13

20 ___ _____

_____

_____

_____

_____

20 ___ _____

_____

_____

_____

_____

20 ___ _____

_____

_____

_____

_____

20 ___ _____

_____

_____

_____

_____

20 ___ _____

_____

_____

_____

_____

AUGUST 14

20 ___ _____
_____
_____
_____
_____

20 ___ _____
_____
_____
_____
_____

20 ___ _____
_____
_____
_____
_____

20 ___ _____
_____
_____
_____
_____

20 ___ _____
_____
_____
_____

AUGUST 15

20 ___ _____

_____

_____

_____

_____

20 ___ _____

_____

_____

_____

_____

20 ___ _____

_____

_____

_____

_____

20 ___ _____

_____

_____

_____

_____

20 ___ _____

_____

_____

_____

_____

AUGUST 16

20 ___ _____

_____

_____

_____

_____

20 ___ _____

_____

_____

_____

_____

20 ___ _____

_____

_____

_____

_____

20 ___ _____

_____

_____

_____

_____

20 ___ _____

_____

_____

_____

_____

AUGUST 17

20 ___ _____
_____
_____
_____
_____

20 ___ _____
_____
_____
_____
_____

20 ___ _____
_____
_____
_____
_____

20 ___ _____
_____
_____
_____
_____

20 ___ _____
_____
_____
_____
_____

AUGUST 18

20 ___ _____

_____

_____

_____

_____

20 ___ _____

_____

_____

_____

_____

20 ___ _____

_____

_____

_____

_____

20 ___ _____

_____

_____

_____

_____

20 ___ _____

_____

_____

_____

_____

AUGUST 19

20 ___ _____

20 ___ _____

20 ___ _____

20 ___ _____

20 ___ _____

AUGUST 20

20 ___ _____

_____

_____

_____

_____

20 ___ _____

_____

_____

_____

_____

20 ___ _____

_____

_____

_____

_____

20 ___ _____

_____

_____

_____

_____

20 ___ _____

_____

_____

_____

_____

AUGUST 21

20 ___ _____

_____

_____

_____

_____

20 ___ _____

_____

_____

_____

_____

20 ___ _____

_____

_____

_____

_____

20 ___ _____

_____

_____

_____

_____

20 ___ _____

_____

_____

_____

_____

AUGUST 22

20 ___ _____

_____

_____

_____

_____

_____

20 ___ _____

_____

_____

_____

_____

_____

20 ___ _____

_____

_____

_____

_____

20 ___ _____

_____

_____

_____

_____

20 ___ _____

_____

_____

_____

_____

AUGUST 23

20 ___ _____
_____
_____
_____
_____
_____

20 ___ _____
_____
_____
_____
_____
_____

20 ___ _____
_____
_____
_____
_____
_____

20 ___ _____
_____
_____
_____
_____
_____

20 ___ _____
_____
_____
_____
_____

AUGUST 24

20 ___ _____

_____

_____

_____

_____

20 ___ _____

_____

_____

_____

_____

20 ___ _____

_____

_____

_____

_____

20 ___ _____

_____

_____

_____

_____

20 ___ _____

_____

_____

_____

_____

AUGUST 25

20 ___ _____

_____

_____

_____

_____

20 ___ _____

_____

_____

_____

_____

20 ___ _____

_____

_____

_____

_____

20 ___ _____

_____

_____

_____

_____

20 ___ _____

_____

_____

_____

_____

AUGUST 26

20 ___ _____

_____

_____

_____

_____

20 ___ _____

_____

_____

_____

_____

20 ___ _____

_____

_____

_____

_____

20 ___ _____

_____

_____

_____

_____

20 ___ _____

_____

_____

_____

_____

AUGUST 27

20 ___ _____

20 ___ _____

20 ___ _____

20 ___ _____

20 ___ _____

AUGUST 28

20 ___ _____

_____

_____

_____

_____

20 ___ _____

_____

_____

_____

_____

20 ___ _____

_____

_____

_____

_____

20 ___ _____

_____

_____

_____

_____

20 ___ _____

_____

_____

_____

_____

AUGUST 29

20 ___ _____

_____

_____

_____

_____

_____

20 ___ _____

_____

_____

_____

_____

_____

20 ___ _____

_____

_____

_____

_____

_____

20 ___ _____

_____

_____

_____

_____

_____

20 ___ _____

_____

_____

_____

_____

_____

AUGUST 30

20 ___ _____

_____

_____

_____

_____

20 ___ _____

_____

_____

_____

_____

20 ___ _____

_____

_____

_____

_____

20 ___ _____

_____

_____

_____

_____

20 ___ _____

_____

_____

_____

_____

AUGUST 31

20 ___ _____

_____

_____

_____

_____

20 ___ _____

_____

_____

_____

_____

20 ___ _____

_____

_____

_____

_____

20 ___ _____

_____

_____

_____

_____

20 ___ _____

_____

_____

_____

_____

SEPTEMBER 1

20 ___ _____

_____

_____

_____

_____

20 ___ _____

_____

_____

_____

_____

20 ___ _____

_____

_____

_____

_____

20 ___ _____

_____

_____

_____

_____

20 ___ _____

_____

_____

_____

_____

SEPTEMBER 2

20 ___ _____
_____
_____
_____
_____

20 ___ _____
_____
_____
_____
_____

20 ___ _____
_____
_____
_____
_____

20 ___ _____
_____
_____
_____
_____

20 ___ _____
_____
_____
_____
_____

SEPTEMBER 3

20 ___ _____

_____

_____

_____

_____

20 ___ _____

_____

_____

_____

_____

20 ___ _____

_____

_____

_____

_____

20 ___ _____

_____

_____

_____

_____

20 ___ _____

_____

_____

_____

_____

SEPTEMBER 4

20 ___ _____

_____

_____

_____

_____

20 ___ _____

_____

_____

_____

_____

20 ___ _____

_____

_____

_____

_____

20 ___ _____

_____

_____

_____

_____

20 ___ _____

_____

_____

_____

_____

SEPTEMBER 5

20 ___ _____

_____

_____

_____

_____

20 ___ _____

_____

_____

_____

_____

20 ___ _____

_____

_____

_____

_____

20 ___ _____

_____

_____

_____

_____

20 ___ _____

_____

_____

_____

_____

SEPTEMBER 6

20 ___ _____

_____

_____

_____

_____

20 ___ _____

_____

_____

_____

_____

20 ___ _____

_____

_____

_____

_____

20 ___ _____

_____

_____

_____

_____

20 ___ _____

_____

_____

_____

_____

SEPTEMBER 7

20 ___ _____

_____

_____

_____

_____

20 ___ _____

_____

_____

_____

_____

20 ___ _____

_____

_____

_____

_____

20 ___ _____

_____

_____

_____

_____

20 ___ _____

_____

_____

_____

_____

SEPTEMBER 8

20 ___ _____

_____

_____

_____

_____

20 ___ _____

_____

_____

_____

_____

20 ___ _____

_____

_____

_____

_____

20 ___ _____

_____

_____

_____

_____

20 ___ _____

_____

_____

_____

_____

SEPTEMBER 9

20 ___ _____

_____

_____

_____

_____

20 ___ _____

_____

_____

_____

_____

20 ___ _____

_____

_____

_____

_____

20 ___ _____

_____

_____

_____

_____

20 ___ _____

_____

_____

_____

_____

SEPTEMBER 10

20 ___ _____

_____

_____

_____

_____

20 ___ _____

_____

_____

_____

_____

20 ___ _____

_____

_____

_____

_____

20 ___ _____

_____

_____

_____

_____

20 ___ _____

_____

_____

_____

_____

SEPTEMBER 11

20 ___ _____
_____
_____
_____
_____

20 ___ _____
_____
_____
_____
_____

20 ___ _____
_____
_____
_____
_____

20 ___ _____
_____
_____
_____
_____

20 ___ _____
_____
_____
_____
_____

SEPTEMBER 12

20 ___ _____

20 ___ _____

20 ___ _____

20 ___ _____

20 ___ _____

SEPTEMBER 13

20 ___ _____

_____

_____

_____

_____

20 ___ _____

_____

_____

_____

_____

20 ___ _____

_____

_____

_____

_____

20 ___ _____

_____

_____

_____

_____

20 ___ _____

_____

_____

_____

_____

SEPTEMBER 14

20 ___ _____

_____

_____

_____

_____

20 ___ _____

_____

_____

_____

_____

20 ___ _____

_____

_____

_____

_____

20 ___ _____

_____

_____

_____

_____

20 ___ _____

_____

_____

_____

_____

SEPTEMBER 15

20 ___ _____

_____

_____

_____

_____

20 ___ _____

_____

_____

_____

_____

20 ___ _____

_____

_____

_____

_____

20 ___ _____

_____

_____

_____

_____

20 ___ _____

_____

_____

_____

_____

SEPTEMBER 16

20 ___ _____

_____

_____

_____

_____

20 ___ _____

_____

_____

_____

_____

20 ___ _____

_____

_____

_____

_____

20 ___ _____

_____

_____

_____

_____

20 ___ _____

_____

_____

_____

_____

SEPTEMBER 17

20 ___ _____
_____
_____
_____
_____

20 ___ _____
_____
_____
_____
_____

20 ___ _____
_____
_____
_____
_____

20 ___ _____
_____
_____
_____
_____

20 ___ _____
_____
_____
_____
_____

SEPTEMBER 18

20 ___ _____

_____

_____

_____

_____

20 ___ _____

_____

_____

_____

_____

20 ___ _____

_____

_____

_____

_____

20 ___ _____

_____

_____

_____

_____

20 ___ _____

_____

_____

_____

_____

SEPTEMBER 19

20 ___ _____

_____

_____

_____

_____

20 ___ _____

_____

_____

_____

_____

20 ___ _____

_____

_____

_____

_____

20 ___ _____

_____

_____

_____

_____

20 ___ _____

_____

_____

_____

_____

SEPTEMBER 20

20 ___ _____

20 ___ _____

20 ___ _____

20 ___ _____

20 ___ _____

SEPTEMBER 21

20 ___ _____

_____

_____

_____

_____

20 ___ _____

_____

_____

_____

_____

20 ___ _____

_____

_____

_____

_____

20 ___ _____

_____

_____

_____

_____

20 ___ _____

_____

_____

_____

_____

SEPTEMBER 22

20 ___ _____

20 ___ _____

20 ___ _____

20 ___ _____

20 ___ _____

SEPTEMBER 23

20 ___ _____

_____

_____

_____

_____

20 ___ _____

_____

_____

_____

_____

20 ___ _____

_____

_____

_____

_____

20 ___ _____

_____

_____

_____

_____

20 ___ _____

_____

_____

_____

_____

SEPTEMBER 24

20 ___ _____

_____

_____

_____

_____

20 ___ _____

_____

_____

_____

_____

20 ___ _____

_____

_____

_____

_____

20 ___ _____

_____

_____

_____

_____

20 ___ _____

_____

_____

_____

_____

SEPTEMBER 25

20 ___ _____

_____

_____

_____

_____

20 ___ _____

_____

_____

_____

_____

20 ___ _____

_____

_____

_____

_____

20 ___ _____

_____

_____

_____

_____

20 ___ _____

_____

_____

_____

_____

SEPTEMBER 26

20 ___ _____

_____

_____

_____

_____

20 ___ _____

_____

_____

_____

_____

20 ___ _____

_____

_____

_____

_____

20 ___ _____

_____

_____

_____

_____

20 ___ _____

_____

_____

_____

_____

SEPTEMBER 27

20 ___ _____

_____

_____

_____

_____

20 ___ _____

_____

_____

_____

_____

20 ___ _____

_____

_____

_____

_____

20 ___ _____

_____

_____

_____

_____

20 ___ _____

_____

_____

_____

_____

SEPTEMBER 28

20 ___ _____

20 ___ _____

20 ___ _____

20 ___ _____

20 ___ _____

SEPTEMBER 29

20 ___ _____

_____

_____

_____

_____

20 ___ _____

_____

_____

_____

_____

20 ___ _____

_____

_____

_____

_____

20 ___ _____

_____

_____

_____

_____

20 ___ _____

_____

_____

_____

_____

SEPTEMBER 30

20 ___ _____

_____

_____

_____

_____

20 ___ _____

_____

_____

_____

_____

20 ___ _____

_____

_____

_____

_____

20 ___ _____

_____

_____

_____

_____

20 ___ _____

_____

_____

_____

_____

OCTOBER 1

20 ___ _____

20 ___ _____

20 ___ _____

20 ___ _____

20 ___ _____

OCTOBER 2

20 ___ _____

_____
_____
_____
_____

20 ___ _____

_____
_____
_____
_____

20 ___ _____

_____
_____
_____
_____

20 ___ _____

_____
_____
_____
_____

20 ___ _____

_____
_____
_____
_____

OCTOBER 3

20 ___ _____

_____

_____

_____

_____

20 ___ _____

_____

_____

_____

_____

20 ___ _____

_____

_____

_____

_____

20 ___ _____

_____

_____

_____

_____

20 ___ _____

_____

_____

_____

_____

OCTOBER 4

20 ___ _____

20 ___ _____

20 ___ _____

20 ___ _____

20 ___ _____

OCTOBER 5

20 ___

_____

_____

_____

_____

20 ___

_____

_____

_____

_____

20 ___

_____

_____

_____

_____

20 ___

_____

_____

_____

_____

20 ___

_____

_____

_____

_____

OCTOBER 6

20 ___ _____

20 ___ _____

20 ___ _____

20 ___ _____

20 ___ _____

OCTOBER 7

20 _____ _____

_____

_____

_____

_____

20 _____ _____

_____

_____

_____

_____

20 _____ _____

_____

_____

_____

_____

20 _____ _____

_____

_____

_____

_____

20 _____ _____

_____

_____

_____

_____

OCTOBER 8

20 ___ _____

20 ___ _____

20 ___ _____

20 ___ _____

20 ___ _____

OCTOBER 9

20 ___ _____

_____

_____

_____

_____

20 ___ _____

_____

_____

_____

_____

20 ___ _____

_____

_____

_____

_____

20 ___ _____

_____

_____

_____

_____

20 ___ _____

_____

_____

_____

_____

OCTOBER 10

20 ___ _____

_____

_____

_____

_____

20 ___ _____

_____

_____

_____

_____

20 ___ _____

_____

_____

_____

_____

20 ___ _____

_____

_____

_____

_____

20 ___ _____

_____

_____

_____

_____

OCTOBER 11

20 ___ _____

_____

_____

_____

_____

20 ___ _____

_____

_____

_____

_____

20 ___ _____

_____

_____

_____

_____

20 ___ _____

_____

_____

_____

_____

20 ___ _____

_____

_____

_____

_____

OCTOBER 12

20 ___ _____
_____
_____
_____
_____

20 ___ _____
_____
_____
_____
_____

20 ___ _____
_____
_____
_____
_____

20 ___ _____
_____
_____
_____
_____

20 ___ _____
_____
_____
_____
_____

OCTOBER 13

20 ___ _____

_____

_____

_____

_____

20 ___ _____

_____

_____

_____

_____

20 ___ _____

_____

_____

_____

_____

20 ___ _____

_____

_____

_____

_____

20 ___ _____

_____

_____

_____

_____

OCTOBER 14

20 ___ _____

_____

_____

_____

_____

20 ___ _____

_____

_____

_____

_____

20 ___ _____

_____

_____

_____

_____

20 ___ _____

_____

_____

_____

_____

20 ___ _____

_____

_____

_____

_____

OCTOBER 15

20 ___ _____

_____

_____

_____

_____

20 ___ _____

_____

_____

_____

_____

20 ___ _____

_____

_____

_____

_____

20 ___ _____

_____

_____

_____

_____

20 ___ _____

_____

_____

_____

_____

OCTOBER 16

20 ___ _____

20 ___ _____

20 ___ _____

20 ___ _____

20 ___ _____

OCTOBER 17

20 _____ _____

_____

_____

_____

_____

20 _____ _____

_____

_____

_____

_____

20 _____ _____

_____

_____

_____

_____

20 _____ _____

_____

_____

_____

_____

20 _____ _____

_____

_____

_____

_____

OCTOBER 18

20 ___ _____

_____

_____

_____

_____

20 ___ _____

_____

_____

_____

_____

20 ___ _____

_____

_____

_____

_____

20 ___ _____

_____

_____

_____

_____

20 ___ _____

_____

_____

_____

_____

OCTOBER 19

20 ___ _____

20 ___ _____

20 ___ _____

20 ___ _____

20 ___ _____

OCTOBER 20

20 ___ _____

_____

_____

_____

_____

20 ___ _____

_____

_____

_____

_____

20 ___ _____

_____

_____

_____

_____

20 ___ _____

_____

_____

_____

_____

20 ___ _____

_____

_____

_____

_____

OCTOBER 21

20 ___ _____

_____

_____

_____

_____

20 ___ _____

_____

_____

_____

_____

20 ___ _____

_____

_____

_____

_____

20 ___ _____

_____

_____

_____

_____

20 ___ _____

_____

_____

_____

_____

OCTOBER 22

20 ___ _____

_____

_____

_____

_____

20 ___ _____

_____

_____

_____

_____

20 ___ _____

_____

_____

_____

_____

20 ___ _____

_____

_____

_____

_____

20 ___ _____

_____

_____

_____

_____

OCTOBER 23

20 ___ _____

_____

_____

_____

_____

20 ___ _____

_____

_____

_____

_____

20 ___ _____

_____

_____

_____

_____

20 ___ _____

_____

_____

_____

_____

20 ___ _____

_____

_____

_____

_____

OCTOBER 24

20 ___ _____
_____
_____
_____
_____
_____

20 ___ _____
_____
_____
_____
_____
_____

20 ___ _____
_____
_____
_____
_____
_____

20 ___ _____
_____
_____
_____
_____
_____

20 ___ _____
_____
_____
_____
_____

OCTOBER 25

20 ___ _____

20 ___ _____

20 ___ _____

20 ___ _____

20 ___ _____

OCTOBER 26

20 ___ _____

_____

_____

_____

_____

20 ___ _____

_____

_____

_____

_____

20 ___ _____

_____

_____

_____

_____

20 ___ _____

_____

_____

_____

_____

20 ___ _____

_____

_____

_____

_____

OCTOBER 27

20 ___ _____

_____

_____

_____

_____

20 ___ _____

_____

_____

_____

_____

20 ___ _____

_____

_____

_____

_____

20 ___ _____

_____

_____

_____

_____

20 ___ _____

_____

_____

_____

_____

OCTOBER 28

20 ___ _____

_____

_____

_____

_____

20 ___ _____

_____

_____

_____

_____

20 ___ _____

_____

_____

_____

_____

20 ___ _____

_____

_____

_____

_____

20 ___ _____

_____

_____

_____

_____

OCTOBER 29

20___

_____

_____

_____

_____

_____

20___

_____

_____

_____

_____

_____

20___

_____

_____

_____

_____

20___

_____

_____

_____

_____

_____

20___

_____

_____

_____

_____

_____

OCTOBER 30

20 ___ _____

_____

_____

_____

_____

20 ___ _____

_____

_____

_____

_____

20 ___ _____

_____

_____

_____

_____

20 ___ _____

_____

_____

_____

_____

20 ___ _____

_____

_____

_____

_____

OCTOBER 31

20 ___ _____

_____

_____

_____

_____

20 ___ _____

_____

_____

_____

_____

20 ___ _____

_____

_____

_____

_____

20 ___ _____

_____

_____

_____

_____

20 ___ _____

_____

_____

_____

_____

NOVEMBER 1

20 ___ _____
_____
_____
_____
_____

20 ___ _____
_____
_____
_____
_____

20 ___ _____
_____
_____
_____
_____

20 ___ _____
_____
_____
_____
_____

20 ___ _____
_____
_____
_____
_____

NOVEMBER 2

20 ___ _____

_____

_____

_____

_____

20 ___ _____

_____

_____

_____

_____

20 ___ _____

_____

_____

_____

_____

20 ___ _____

_____

_____

_____

_____

20 ___ _____

_____

_____

_____

_____

NOVEMBER 3

20 ___ _____
_____
_____
_____
_____

20 ___ _____
_____
_____
_____
_____

20 ___ _____
_____
_____
_____
_____

20 ___ _____
_____
_____
_____
_____

20 ___ _____
_____
_____
_____
_____

NOVEMBER 4

20 ___ _____
_____
_____
_____
_____
_____

20 ___ _____
_____
_____
_____
_____
_____

20 ___ _____
_____
_____
_____
_____
_____

20 ___ _____
_____
_____
_____
_____
_____

20 ___ _____
_____
_____
_____
_____
_____

NOVEMBER 5

20 ___ _____

_____

_____

_____

_____

20 ___ _____

_____

_____

_____

_____

20 ___ _____

_____

_____

_____

_____

20 ___ _____

_____

_____

_____

_____

20 ___ _____

_____

_____

_____

_____

NOVEMBER 6

20 ___ _____

_____

_____

_____

_____

_____

20 ___ _____

_____

_____

_____

_____

_____

20 ___ _____

_____

_____

_____

_____

_____

20 ___ _____

_____

_____

_____

_____

_____

20 ___ _____

_____

_____

_____

_____

NOVEMBER 7

20 ___ _____

_____

_____

_____

_____

20 ___ _____

_____

_____

_____

_____

20 ___ _____

_____

_____

_____

_____

20 ___ _____

_____

_____

_____

_____

20 ___ _____

_____

_____

_____

_____

NOVEMBER 8

20 ___ _____

_____

_____

_____

_____

20 ___ _____

_____

_____

_____

_____

20 ___ _____

_____

_____

_____

_____

20 ___ _____

_____

_____

_____

_____

20 ___ _____

_____

_____

_____

_____

NOVEMBER 9

20 ___ _____

20 ___ _____

20 ___ _____

20 ___ _____

20 ___ _____

NOVEMBER 10

20 _____ _____
_____
_____
_____
_____

20 _____ _____
_____
_____
_____
_____

20 _____ _____
_____
_____
_____
_____

20 _____ _____
_____
_____
_____
_____

20 _____ _____
_____
_____
_____
_____

NOVEMBER 11

20 ___ _____
_____
_____
_____
_____

20 ___ _____
_____
_____
_____
_____

20 ___ _____
_____
_____
_____
_____

20 ___ _____
_____
_____
_____
_____

20 ___ _____
_____
_____
_____
_____

NOVEMBER 12

20 ___ _____
_____
_____
_____
_____

20 ___ _____
_____
_____
_____
_____

20 ___ _____
_____
_____
_____
_____

20 ___ _____
_____
_____
_____
_____

20 ___ _____
_____
_____
_____
_____

NOVEMBER 13

20 ___ _____
_____
_____
_____
_____

20 ___ _____
_____
_____
_____
_____

20 ___ _____
_____
_____
_____
_____

20 ___ _____
_____
_____
_____
_____

20 ___ _____
_____
_____
_____
_____

NOVEMBER 14

20 ___ _____

_____

_____

_____

_____

20 ___ _____

_____

_____

_____

_____

20 ___ _____

_____

_____

_____

_____

20 ___ _____

_____

_____

_____

_____

20 ___ _____

_____

_____

_____

_____

NOVEMBER 15

20 ___ _____

20 ___ _____

20 ___ _____

20 ___ _____

20 ___ _____

NOVEMBER 16

20 ___ _____

_____

_____

_____

_____

20 ___ _____

_____

_____

_____

_____

20 ___ _____

_____

_____

_____

_____

20 ___ _____

_____

_____

_____

_____

20 ___ _____

_____

_____

_____

_____

NOVEMBER 17

20 ___ _____

20 ___ _____

20 ___ _____

20 ___ _____

20 ___ _____

NOVEMBER 18

20 ___ _____

_____

_____

_____

_____

20 ___ _____

_____

_____

_____

_____

20 ___ _____

_____

_____

_____

_____

20 ___ _____

_____

_____

_____

_____

20 ___ _____

_____

_____

_____

_____

NOVEMBER 19

20 ___ _____

_____

_____

_____

_____

20 ___ _____

_____

_____

_____

_____

20 ___ _____

_____

_____

_____

_____

20 ___ _____

_____

_____

_____

_____

20 ___ _____

_____

_____

_____

_____

NOVEMBER 20

20 ___ _____

_____
_____
_____
_____

20 ___ _____

_____
_____
_____
_____

20 ___ _____

_____
_____
_____
_____

20 ___ _____

_____
_____
_____
_____

20 ___ _____

_____
_____
_____
_____

NOVEMBER 21

20 ___ _____
_____
_____
_____
_____

20 ___ _____
_____
_____
_____
_____

20 ___ _____
_____
_____
_____
_____

20 ___ _____
_____
_____
_____
_____

20 ___ _____
_____
_____
_____
_____

NOVEMBER 22

20 ___

_____

_____

_____

_____

_____

20 ___

_____

_____

_____

_____

_____

20 ___

_____

_____

_____

_____

_____

20 ___

_____

_____

_____

_____

_____

20 ___

_____

_____

_____

_____

_____

NOVEMBER 23

20 ___

_____

_____

_____

_____

_____

20 ___

_____

_____

_____

_____

_____

20 ___

_____

_____

_____

_____

_____

20 ___

_____

_____

_____

_____

_____

20 ___

_____

_____

_____

_____

_____

NOVEMBER 24

20 ___ _____

_____

_____

_____

_____

20 ___ _____

_____

_____

_____

_____

20 ___ _____

_____

_____

_____

_____

20 ___ _____

_____

_____

_____

_____

20 ___ _____

_____

_____

_____

_____

NOVEMBER 25

20 ___ _____

20 ___ _____

20 ___ _____

20 ___ _____

20 ___ _____

NOVEMBER 26

20 ___ _____

_____

_____

_____

_____

20 ___ _____

_____

_____

_____

_____

20 ___ _____

_____

_____

_____

_____

20 ___ _____

_____

_____

_____

_____

20 ___ _____

_____

_____

_____

_____

NOVEMBER 27

20 ___ _____

_____

_____

_____

_____

20 ___ _____

_____

_____

_____

_____

20 ___ _____

_____

_____

_____

_____

20 ___ _____

_____

_____

_____

_____

20 ___ _____

_____

_____

_____

_____

NOVEMBER 28

20 ___ _____

_____

_____

_____

20 ___ _____

_____

_____

_____

20 ___ _____

_____

_____

_____

20 ___ _____

_____

_____

_____

20 ___ _____

_____

_____

_____

NOVEMBER 29

20 ___ _____
_____
_____
_____
_____

20 ___ _____
_____
_____
_____
_____

20 ___ _____
_____
_____
_____
_____

20 ___ _____
_____
_____
_____
_____

20 ___ _____
_____
_____
_____
_____

NOVEMBER 30

20 ___ _____

_____

_____

_____

_____

20 ___ _____

_____

_____

_____

_____

20 ___ _____

_____

_____

_____

_____

20 ___ _____

_____

_____

_____

_____

20 ___ _____

_____

_____

_____

_____

DECEMBER 1

20 ___ _____

_____

_____

_____

_____

20 ___ _____

_____

_____

_____

_____

20 ___ _____

_____

_____

_____

_____

20 ___ _____

_____

_____

_____

_____

20 ___ _____

_____

_____

_____

_____

DECEMBER 2

20 ___ _____

_____

_____

_____

_____

20 ___ _____

_____

_____

_____

_____

20 ___ _____

_____

_____

_____

_____

20 ___ _____

_____

_____

_____

_____

20 ___ _____

_____

_____

_____

_____

DECEMBER 3

20 ___ _____

_____

_____

_____

_____

_____

20 ___ _____

_____

_____

_____

_____

_____

20 ___ _____

_____

_____

_____

_____

_____

20 ___ _____

_____

_____

_____

_____

_____

20 ___ _____

_____

_____

_____

_____

_____

DECEMBER 4

20 ___ _____
_____
_____
_____
_____

20 ___ _____
_____
_____
_____
_____

20 ___ _____
_____
_____
_____
_____

20 ___ _____
_____
_____
_____
_____

20 ___ _____
_____
_____
_____
_____

DECEMBER 5

20 ___ _____
_____
_____
_____
_____

20 ___ _____
_____
_____
_____
_____

20 ___ _____
_____
_____
_____
_____

20 ___ _____
_____
_____
_____
_____

20 ___ _____
_____
_____
_____
_____

DECEMBER 6

20 ___ _____
_____
_____
_____
_____

20 ___ _____
_____
_____
_____
_____

20 ___ _____
_____
_____
_____
_____

20 ___ _____
_____
_____
_____
_____

20 ___ _____
_____
_____
_____
_____

DECEMBER 7

20 ___ _____

_____

_____

_____

_____

20 ___ _____

_____

_____

_____

_____

20 ___ _____

_____

_____

_____

_____

20 ___ _____

_____

_____

_____

_____

20 ___ _____

_____

_____

_____

_____

DECEMBER 8

20 ___ _____

_____

_____

_____

_____

20 ___ _____

_____

_____

_____

_____

20 ___ _____

_____

_____

_____

_____

20 ___ _____

_____

_____

_____

_____

20 ___ _____

_____

_____

_____

_____

DECEMBER 9

20 ___ _____

_____

_____

_____

_____

20 ___ _____

_____

_____

_____

_____

20 ___ _____

_____

_____

_____

_____

20 ___ _____

_____

_____

_____

_____

20 ___ _____

_____

_____

_____

_____

DECEMBER 10

20 ___ _____

20 ___ _____

20 ___ _____

20 ___ _____

20 ___ _____

DECEMBER 11

20 ___ _____
_____
_____
_____
_____
_____

20 ___ _____
_____
_____
_____
_____
_____

20 ___ _____
_____
_____
_____
_____
_____

20 ___ _____
_____
_____
_____
_____
_____

20 ___ _____
_____
_____
_____
_____
_____

DECEMBER 12

20 ___ _____

_____

_____

_____

_____

20 ___ _____

_____

_____

_____

_____

20 ___ _____

_____

_____

_____

_____

20 ___ _____

_____

_____

_____

_____

20 ___ _____

_____

_____

_____

_____

DECEMBER 13

20 ___ _____

_____

_____

_____

_____

20 ___ _____

_____

_____

_____

_____

20 ___ _____

_____

_____

_____

_____

20 ___ _____

_____

_____

_____

_____

20 ___ _____

_____

_____

_____

_____

DECEMBER 14

20 ___

20 ___

20 ___

20 ___

20 ___

DECEMBER 15

20 ___ _____

_____

_____

_____

_____

20 ___ _____

_____

_____

_____

_____

20 ___ _____

_____

_____

_____

_____

20 ___ _____

_____

_____

_____

_____

20 ___ _____

_____

_____

_____

_____

DECEMBER 16

20 ___ _____

_____

_____

_____

_____

20 ___ _____

_____

_____

_____

_____

20 ___ _____

_____

_____

_____

_____

20 ___ _____

_____

_____

_____

_____

20 ___ _____

_____

_____

_____

_____

DECEMBER 17

20 ___ _____

_____

_____

_____

_____

20 ___ _____

_____

_____

_____

_____

20 ___ _____

_____

_____

_____

_____

20 ___ _____

_____

_____

_____

_____

20 ___ _____

_____

_____

_____

_____

DECEMBER 18

20 ___ _____

20 ___ _____

20 ___ _____

20 ___ _____

20 ___ _____

DECEMBER 19

20 ___ _____

_____

_____

_____

_____

20 ___ _____

_____

_____

_____

_____

20 ___ _____

_____

_____

_____

_____

20 ___ _____

_____

_____

_____

_____

20 ___ _____

_____

_____

_____

_____

DECEMBER 20

20 ___ _____

_____

_____

_____

_____

20 ___ _____

_____

_____

_____

_____

20 ___ _____

_____

_____

_____

_____

20 ___ _____

_____

_____

_____

_____

20 ___ _____

_____

_____

_____

_____

DECEMBER 21

20 ___ _____

20 ___ _____

20 ___ _____

20 ___ _____

20 ___ _____

DECEMBER 22

20 ___ _____

_____

_____

_____

_____

_____

20 ___ _____

_____

_____

_____

_____

_____

20 ___ _____

_____

_____

_____

_____

_____

20 ___ _____

_____

_____

_____

_____

_____

20 ___ _____

_____

_____

_____

_____

_____

DECEMBER 23

20 ___ _____

_____

_____

_____

_____

20 ___ _____

_____

_____

_____

_____

20 ___ _____

_____

_____

_____

_____

20 ___ _____

_____

_____

_____

_____

20 ___ _____

_____

_____

_____

_____

DECEMBER 24

20 ___ _____

_____

_____

_____

_____

20 ___ _____

_____

_____

_____

_____

20 ___ _____

_____

_____

_____

_____

20 ___ _____

_____

_____

_____

_____

20 ___ _____

_____

_____

_____

_____

DECEMBER 25

20 ___ _____

20 ___ _____

20 ___ _____

20 ___ _____

20 ___ _____

DECEMBER 26

20 ___ _____

20 ___ _____

20 ___ _____

20 ___ _____

20 ___ _____

DECEMBER 27

20 ___ _____

_____

_____

_____

_____

20 ___ _____

_____

_____

_____

_____

20 ___ _____

_____

_____

_____

_____

20 ___ _____

_____

_____

_____

_____

20 ___ _____

_____

_____

_____

_____

DECEMBER 28

20 __ _____
_____
_____
_____
_____
_____

20 __ _____
_____
_____
_____
_____
_____

20 __ _____
_____
_____
_____
_____
_____

20 __ _____
_____
_____
_____
_____
_____

20 __ _____
_____
_____
_____
_____
_____

DECEMBER 29

20 ___ _____

20 ___ _____

20 ___ _____

20 ___ _____

20 ___ _____

DECEMBER 30

20 ___ _____

_____

_____

_____

_____

20 ___ _____

_____

_____

_____

_____

20 ___ _____

_____

_____

_____

_____

20 ___ _____

_____

_____

_____

_____

20 ___ _____

_____

_____

_____

_____

DECEMBER 31

20 ___ _____

_____

_____

_____

_____

20 ___ _____

_____

_____

_____

_____

20 ___ _____

_____

_____

_____

_____

20 ___ _____

_____

_____

_____

_____

20 ___ _____

_____

_____

_____

_____

DATES TO REMEMBER

DATES TO REMEMBER

_____
_____
_____
_____
_____
_____
_____
_____
_____
_____
_____
_____
_____
_____
_____
_____
_____
_____
_____
_____
_____
_____
_____